seventeen

presents...

MEGA

traumarama!

Real Girls and Guys Confess More of Their Most Mortifying Moments!

seventeen
presents...

MEGA
traumarama!

Real Girls and Guys Confess More of Their **Most Mortifying** Moments!

From the Editors of
seventeen Magazine

HEARST BOOKS
A division of Sterling Publishing Co., Inc.

New York / London
www.sterlingpublishing.com

Library of Congress Cataloging-in-Publication Data

Seventeen's mega traumarama! : real girls and guys confess
more of their most mortifying moments! / from the editors of
Seventeen Magazine ; illustrations by Chuck Gonzalez.
       p. cm.
   Includes index.
   ISBN 978-1-58816-730-9
   1. Teenagers—United States—Social conditions. 2. Young
adults—United States—Social conditions. 3. Embarrassment
in adolescence—United States. I. Seventeen.
   HQ796S437 2008
   155.5'1240973—dc22
                                    2008018779

10 9 8 7 6 5 4 3 2 1

Seventeen and Hearst Books are trademarks of
Hearst Communications, Inc.

www.seventeen.com

For information about custom editions, special sales,
premium and corporate purchases, please contact
Sterling Special Sales Department at 800-805-5489
or specialsales@sterlingpublishing.com.

Distributed in Canada by Sterling Publishing
c/o Canadian Manda Group, 165 Dufferin Street
Toronto, Ontario, Canada M6K 3H6

Distributed in Australia by Capricorn Link (Australia) Pty. Ltd.,
P.O. Box 704, Windsor, NSW 2756 Australia

Printed in China

Sterling ISBN 978-1-58816-730-9

see page
14

see page
69

see page
123

see page
213

contents

Hi from Ann 8

Chapter 1 CRUSH 11

Chapter 2 FAMILY 65

Chapter 3 FRIENDS 119

Chapter 4 SCHOOL 163

Chapter 5 FASHION 207

Index 252

see page 95

see page 41

see page 137

CLEANING SOLUTION

see page 237

Hi!

You know how our motto is It's Fun to Be Seventeen? Well, there is almost nothing that's more fun than reading someone *else's* most embarrassing moments. (Of course, when it happens to you, you want to hide from the world... until you realize that it's actually a pretty funny story to share!) While working at *Seventeen*, I've been reading (and dying laughing) at your traumaramas for years, so it's only fair that I share mine now. Laugh away!

> I was walking down a busy street in Manhattan one day feeling **awesome**. I had on a cute outfit and my hair was doing all the right things...then suddenly my feet went out from under me and I went **flying** across the pavement and slammed into the

window of a giant skyscraper. When I peeled myself off the glass and looked around to see who had pushed me, the only thing I could see was a **banana peel** in the middle of the sidewalk. Who slips on a banana peel in real life? I tried to play it off like it was no big deal (people were staring!) but both my entire left side and my ego were **majorly** bruised!

Hey, humiliating moments happen to *everyone* (even editors-in-chief)!

xoxo
— A.

Ann Shoket
Editor-in-Chief
seventeen

"I decided to flush it down the toilet and hope for the best"

see page 24

crush

The most **extreme** embarrassment:
IFOC (in front of **crush**).

crush

crushing blow

" Last year after Thanksgiving dinner, we decided to play some football outside. The **teams** were my cute neighbor and me versus my brother and my cousin. My cute neighbor threw the ball to me—but instead of catching it, I got hit in the **face**! If that wasn't embarrassing enough, my nose started **bleeding**. So much for impressing my crush with my skills! "

catch of the day

"I was fishing with my cousin and some of his guy friends when I felt a huge tug on my line. I starting **screaming** so the guys would notice. Just as they were looking, I lost my **balance** and fell into the cold lake. They pulled me out, along with the **fish**— which was only five inches long!"

crush

go fish

"My boyfriend took me to SeaWorld, and we decided to go see the seals. He left and came back with a **tray** of fish to feed them. While I was tossing out the fish, my boyfriend stepped back to take a picture, and all of a sudden this **huge** bird flew toward me. It wanted the **fish**—and basically attacked me to get them! My boyfriend was laughing his head off. He got a hilarious **picture** of it all that he still has today and shows everyone."

rush

movie pass

"One night I was at the movies with some friends, and a **cute** guy behind the snack counter was totally checking me out! We decided to split a jumbo-size soda so we could keep going back for free **refills**. When it was my turn to go up to the counter, he asked me, 'Can you take your top off?' I immediately shouted back, 'No way!' He then clarified, 'Can you take the lid off?' I couldn't believe I had **completely** misunderstood him. I was so humiliated!"

getaway car

"I was hanging out with my crush outside of Starbucks, waiting for our parents to pick us up. My mom's **car** pulled into the parking lot, so I hopped in the car. As I **buckled** my seat belt, the lady in the driver's seat asked, 'Uh, who are you?' I freaked out and was like, 'I'm so sorry! I thought you were my **mom**!' I jumped out, and the lady drove off really fast. My crush started cracking up and making fun of me. At least he had a good laugh!"

tissue issue

"I was talking with my friend and my crush when I started **laughing** hysterically at something my friend had said. All of a sudden, a huge snot flew out of my nose! Hoping my crush hadn't noticed, I **quickly** excused myself and got a tissue. But when I came back, he was almost **falling** out of his seat cracking up. I wanted to die."

exchange policy

"One time my friends and I went to a school conference and we met this really **cute** guy. After we'd talked awhile, he asked for my contact info. I pulled a **receipt** out of my bag to write down my MySpace address. When I handed it to him, he just looked at it and **laughed**. I had no idea what was so funny until he showed it to me—it was a receipt for a box of **tampons**!"

crush

GUY trauma

closet case

> During my junior year I stayed in the dorms. One night after taking a fast **shower**, as I was walking to my bedroom, all my friends jumped on me and pulled off my **towel**! They shoved me out of the room—buck naked. Then one of them started knocking on **all** the doors on our floor. Everyone—guys *and* girls—came running out of their rooms to see what was going on. I was so embarrassed that I ran and **hid** in the utility closet on our floor!

crush

paper trail

" I was at a party at my grandma's house, and my cousin brought his **hot** best friend. We were flirting all night, and after dinner the two of us went for a **walk** around the neighborhood alone. He **leaned** in toward my face, and I thought he was getting ready to kiss me. Instead he **whispered** in my ear, 'You've been walking around with toilet paper stuck to your skirt for about an hour.' I wanted to go in a corner and cry. "

gotta jet

"I was on a plane when I noticed this hot guy three rows behind me. I really had to pass gas but I knew it would smell bad, so I went to the **restroom**. When I opened the door, the hot guy was **waiting** to use the bathroom after me. Back at my seat, I noticed he hadn't shut the door yet. Instead he walked out, gave me a **weird** look, and walked to the other restroom on the **opposite** side of the plane. I was mortified!"

plumber bummer

"I had to change my pad one day at my boyfriend's house, but there was no trash can in the bathroom. I decided to **flush** it down the toilet and hope for the best. Everything was fine until my **boyfriend** went to the bathroom. When he flushed the toilet, it clogged. He got a **plunger**, and up popped my pad! What made it worse was that he knew it was mine—he has a family full of **boys**, and there were no other girls in his house. It was so humiliating."

gym-nauseam

"I knew my crush's **schedule** as well as my own, so I planned to 'run into' him at the gym. I was on the treadmill when I started to get **cramps**, but I ignored them and just kept going. My crush came over, saw my incline, and said he was impressed. Then he asked how long I could keep going. I was about to **open** my mouth to say, 'Forty-five minutes,' when my **stomach** let out a roar and I vomited all over him! I really wanted to die!"

crush

you got served

"I had just started lessons with a new tennis **instructor**, and he was really hot. During one of our sessions, I decided to **impress** him with my moves. So I served the ball to him with all my strength— and it hit him in the **face**. Later I found out I'd broken his nose! Oops."

crush

stopping traffic

"I was at the mall looking for a parking spot. I saw one and made my friend hop out of the car to save it until I could get in a **position** to back in. At that moment a truck of really cute guys drove by, and they **shouted** something to us. I smiled at them, but I was so **distracted** that I backed into a pole! The guys saw the whole thing, burst into laughter, and drove away."

mobile chat

"I was on the bus, and I'd snagged a seat right next to my crush. I was so **excited** when he said, 'Hey,' so I started talking to him. But then he **turned** and gave me a really weird look. That was when I noticed he had a Bluetooth phone headset on and had been talking to **someone** else the whole time. I was so **embarrassed**, I got off at the next bus stop even though it wasn't mine!"

lovesick

"

I was at the county fair with my crush. We were having a **great** time with each other. We ate lunch and then decided to go on this ride called The Zipper. But when we got off, I felt sick to my stomach. Just then he **leaned** in to kiss me, and my *worst* nightmare happened—I threw up! It was **seriously** the most embarrassing moment of my life.

"

hide-and-peek

"I was browsing through magazines at the mall bookstore with my friends and saw my crush. I got really **shy** and didn't want him to see me, so I grabbed something off the rack and pretended to read it to **hide** my face. Then I heard my friends and my crush **laughing**. When I looked over the edge of the page, they were all pointing at my reading material. I wondered why until I saw that the **magazine** I was holding was *Playboy*!"

crush

off the rack

> My friends and I were at the **mall** when we saw a hot guy working at a CD store. We went in and flirted with him a little. The manager kept glaring at us, so I pretended I was looking at CDs. I **leaned** on a rack behind me to look cool, but it wasn't bolted into the ground. Everything **fell**, including me. I looked up from the middle of the pile, only to see my friends bolt. They left me there to face the hot guy and his boss!

GUY trauma

numbers game

" I was with a friend when I bumped into this girl I had a crush on. I could tell she liked me, so I asked for her phone number. She quickly wrote it down and gave me a **sweet** smile as she walked away. Something made me look up at the awning of the **pizzeria** we were standing in front of. The number she had just given me was the **same** as the pizzeria's! All I could do was laugh at myself. "

lost and found

"When I was younger, my front tooth fell out after an accident, so I got a fake one to replace it. Well, one day at school I was talking to this guy, and when I opened my mouth, I felt **something** but didn't know what it was, so I just kept talking. He looked at me with a shocked expression and asked me, 'Um, **where** did your tooth go?' It got worse when I tried to find it and he said, 'Here it is,' pointing to a small white thing—my tooth!—on his shoe. I was seriously mortified."

mixed messages

"

I was in gym class, and I realized I didn't have an extra maxi pad, which I really needed. So I **texted** my mom and asked if she could bring me something. I wrote, 'I need a tampon or pad because I'm leaking a lot.' A few minutes later I got a text from my **boyfriend** that said, 'Alright. . . .' I was really confused at first. Then I **realized** that I had sent my tampon plea to *him*!

"

cyber slipup

"I was IMing the guy I liked when my **favorite** show, *Sex and the City*, came on. I got so excited that I IM'd him, 'I LOVE SEX!'—I was *trying* to tell him I loved the **show**, but I'd pressed 'enter' too quickly. He IM'd me back, 'Uh . . . well, that's great.' I was so **embarrassed**, I told him I had to leave— and I didn't talk to him again for a week!"

clear view

"Our house has a really nice master bathroom on the second floor, with **huge** windows and no curtains or blinds. One day I was sitting in our yard, when my hot neighbor came over to chat. I was totally **flattered** and thought the conversation was going well, when he said, 'You should probably cover your windows. It's easy to see into them at night.' Apparently the **entire** neighborhood could see me in the nude whenever I took a bath!"

wrong call

"My friend and I were at an event, and this cute guy kept **staring** at us. He came over after my friend left, and we started to talk. I was **flirting** with him as hard as he was with **me**, but then he said, 'Your friend's hot—think she'll give me her number?' I was *humiliated*!"

crush

mud bath

"I was on a date with a really hot guy, and we were walking through the woods to get to this **romantic** spot where there's a bench and green grass. We were almost there when he went in for a kiss. I was so **shocked** that I had to move my foot for better balance—and I put it down right in a mud puddle. My foot slipped, and I fell down into the **dirty** water! Let's just say all the romance was gone once I was covered in muck."

the deep end

"My friend and I were at the pool, and I saw this totally **cute** guy looking at me. I decided to show off for him by doing a **fancy** move from the diving board. But as soon as I put one foot on the board, every single lifeguard at the pool bolted toward me—one even put a **siren** on—and chased me off! It turns out no one was allowed to go near the diving board. The cute guy was **laughing** his head off! It was so embarrassing."

making moves

"I was on a date at a restaurant. Out of habit, I put my feet on the bar under the **table**. Well, like 10 minutes later, the **bar** moved. I looked down and realized it was my date's *feet*—he thought I was playing footsie! He was totally **embarrassed** since it was only our second date—he probably thought I was being really forward. It was awful!"

crush

send-off

" I was in the auditorium for drama practice one afternoon when my **crush** walked over to me and asked for my e-mail address. I couldn't believe it! I was so excited that he was interested in me, so I flashed him this **flirty** smile and I asked for his e-mail too. But he quickly explained that he was asking for *everyone's* e-mail so that he could send us **rehearsal** notices—and then walked away without giving me his info! I felt like such a loser. "

my two scents

"Everything was going great at my school's holiday party last year. We were **finally** going to find out who our Secret Santas were. We **all** exchanged presents, and when I opened mine, I couldn't believe it: I got deodorant and body spray! Worst of all, it came from my **crush**. I felt completely mortified!"

crush

ornamental oops!

"This guy I really liked invited me to his house. His family put a lot of work into decorating their Christmas tree, so I asked if I could see it. There was one **really** beautiful ornament and when I went to touch it, it just broke into **tiny** pieces. His parents were so upset, they looked like they were going to yell at us! When we left, he told me that the ornament had been passed on through the **years** by his grandmother who had just died."

gym class hero

"There was this really cute guy lifting **weights** in PE. To impress him, I decided I'd bench 100 pounds. But as I lifted the bar, I dropped it. I **yelled** for help, and he came over to pull it off me. After the **rescue**, he went over to his friends and laughed at me!"

fall sport

" It was my first day of tennis class and there were a few really cute guys watching from the **bleachers**. While I was playing in my first match, I caught one of them watching me, so I tried to show off my skills and **win** the point. But as I was running toward the ball, I tripped and **fell** flat on my butt I lay on the court for a few seconds, **humiliated**, hoping the guys hadn't seen. Of course when I sat up, they were laughing hysterically! "

foot bawl

> I went over to my boyfriend's house the other day. He put on this new CD so I could hear it, and I sat down to take off my **sneakers**. I stuck my shoes under his bed and walked over to where he was. When I got next to him, he looked at me and was like, 'You know what you need?' Being **cute**, I said, 'A kiss?' But then he just started laughing and said, 'No—foot spray!' and **actually** got out his Odor-Eaters spray can. I could have died.

spitting distance

"My guy and I went on a fast, spinning ride at the carnival, and I was **screaming** the entire time we were on it. When the ride **stopped**, my boyfriend told me that my saliva had been flying out of my mouth and onto his face the **whole** time! Ouch."

crush

puddle jumper

"One day my ex and his new girlfriend came into the restaurant where I work. To make him **jealous**, I went over to my new boyfriend at another table. I started **flirting** with him and laughing to make it look like I was having fun. During my little act I didn't realize the floor had been freshly mopped, and just as I passed my ex's table, I **slipped** and fell right on my butt! His new girlfriend said, 'I can't believe you went out with that girl!' I was humiliated."

52

crush

mr. sensitivity

"The girl I liked invited me over to watch a movie. When she popped in *Miss Congeniality*, I figured this was my chance to show my softer side, but I found myself enjoying it *way* more than she did. Something about it just made me tear up! When my crush saw my face, she pushed me away and said, 'Dude, are you *crying*?' Apparently I was a little *too* sensitive for her liking. The minute the movie ended, she could barely stifle her laughter as she showed me to the door."

total phone-y

"So my friend and I were at the park, and these guys were looking at us. Finally they came over to **talk**. We fake-flirted with them for a while and said we had to go. We thought we'd be smart and give them our fake 'rejection' **numbers**. Later, though, we changed our minds about the guys and tried to call them up. It turns out they'd given **us** fake numbers too!"

crush

surprise surprise

"I was at my boyfriend's house just goofing off—and at some point, we started wrestling. As a special attack move, he started **tickling** me. I was totally surprised, and I laughed so hard that I farted right in his face! He stopped **laughing** and gave me this look. I tried to play it off like it was no big deal, but the rest of the day was a little **awkward**!"

she bangs

"One day my crush was dropping me off at my house. I didn't know if I should **kiss** him or not, so I opened the car door in a hurry so there wouldn't be any **awkwardness**. After I got out, he said my name in a really cute voice, and I **thought** he wanted a kiss. So I started leaning back in with a huge smile when he said, 'You do realize that you just hit your family's mailbox with my door, don't you?' I felt so **totally** dumb!"

sounding off

"I'd just moved to Arizona, and I kept hearing about this band at my new school—and how bad their singer was. I found out that the guy I **liked** was in the band, so one day I got up the **courage** to go up and talk to him. I said, 'From what I hear, your band needs a new singer!' He gave me this **weird** look and was like, 'Uh . . . I am the singer!' I felt terrible!"

eye browse

"When I finally got to meet my boyfriend's family, I wanted to make a good **impression**. So we're sitting in his parents' house, and his mom says, 'Are you spending the night here with us?' I told her I wasn't, and she told me that she was talking to her son. I **apologized** and said that I thought she was looking at me when she asked. The room got really **quiet**, and my boyfriend later explained that she's blind in one eye and sometimes it wanders. I was **mortified**—I wish he'd told me earlier."

crush

blowout

"

It was my first date **ever** with a boy, and I had a slight cold. We went to a nice restaurant, and while we were eating our meal, I **sneezed**—and a huge booger bubble came out of my nose! It was awful, and it *wouldn't* go away. I jumped up as fast as I could and **ran** to the bathroom with my hands over my face. After that, the guy never asked to go anywhere with me again. It was so horrible!

"

crush

GUY trauma

food fight

" During a layover at the airport, I bought a magazine and a Kit Kat bar. I sat down and put the candy on the seat beside me. When a guy sat down nearby, he put his muffin with my Kit Kat. Every few minutes I'd take a bite, and every time, this guy would take a bite of my chocolate too! When he ate the *last* piece, I got angry: I threw the wrapper at him, crushed his muffin, and left. Later, I found my Kit Kat bar in my pocket! "

candid camera

"I sent my crush an instant message to set up a video **chat**. As I waited for the camera to load, I sat there and casually rubbed—okay, picked!—my nose. After **waiting** five minutes, I figured that the camera wasn't working so I typed, 'Too bad, I guess it didn't work!' To my **horror**, he replied: 'It worked all right. I could see you— I just couldn't hear your voice.' I sat there in **panic**, not knowing what to do. Then he typed: 'Don't worry, I think you got that booger out!'"

"...I smelled something awful and realized I had set my hair on fire!"

see page 68

family

Why do our **relatives** always seem to **mortify** the ones they love?

family

merry mistake

"My new boyfriend and I were heading over to a family Christmas party to say hello, and my aunt's friend, who'd just had a baby, was there. She had the infant in her arms, so I automatically went over to **play** with the baby. It wasn't until she said, 'I'll be done feeding her and then you can see her,' that I **realized** she was breast-feeding! Everyone **heard** what happened and started cracking up—ugh!"

ho, ho, oh, no!

"My dad and I were baking cookies one day around Christmas when he **proclaimed** himself the Master Baker. Since I was the one doing **all** the work, I asked why he got to be the Master Bator. Then I realized what had **slipped** out and said, 'I mean, Master Baker, Master Baker!' I ran out of the room—I was so embarrassed."

all fired up

" At a family gathering on Christmas Eve, I took on the duty of blowing out all the **candles** before we went to bed. When I bent down to blow one out, my **hair** caught fire! My cousin ran over and pushed me to the floor to put it out. Luckily my hair was fine, but it **smelled**.
I was mortified. "

family

monitor mishap

" On Thanksgiving we had invited my whole family and some friends, including my parents' friends' **hot** son. When we heard my baby niece crying, my sister and I went to go check on her. While we were in the room, I told my sister how funny and cute I thought my crush was. When we walked back into the living room, **everybody** started cracking up. It turns out that the baby monitor was **on**, so they had heard all the things I told my sister! I could feel myself turning bright red. **"**

icy reception

" I invited my cute guy friend to a ski resort with us over winter break. We were **joking** around one day, and my sister hit me in the back of my head with a snowball. It hurt so badly that I started tearing up. My crush just looked at me like I was a **baby**. I later got back at my sis by doing the same thing, except she really **did** cry—and he told me I was mean! Needless to say, the relationship didn't work out like I'd hoped. "

family

thanks a lot

"Last year we went to my grandma's house for Thanksgiving dinner. She invited the neighbors, and I had a **huge** crush on their son. But I must have had some kind of **reaction** to something I ate because just as we were getting up from the table, I threw up! I felt so embarrassed and **hid** in the bathroom for the rest of the night."

dinner disaster

"It was Thanksgiving, and my **whole** family and my boyfriend were sitting down eating dinner. When my guy asked me to pass the gravy, it slipped out of my hand and **spilled** all over his lap. Everyone started laughing, so I laughed along with them, but then I let out a huge fart by accident! I was so **mortified** that I didn't talk to him for the rest of the night."

a holiday hit

" I had **just** received my driver's permit, so my mom let me drive to my grandparents' house for a family gathering. As I was parking in their driveway, I got **nervous** and accidentally slammed on the gas instead of the brake! I hit my uncle's car, which lunged into the garage door. Thankfully no one was hurt, and everyone was really nice about it. I stayed in the car and **cried** for a half hour, and I couldn't look anyone in the eye for the rest of the night! "

festival of fright

> My mother invited a bunch of family and friends to our Hanukkah party, including a guy I liked. My parents kept **pushing** me to light the candles and do the blessings. I was afraid to sing in front of my **crush**, but my parents were relentless, so I finally gave in. I began to say the blessings, but I was so **nervous** that I started to say completely the wrong one! I even lit the candles in the **wrong** direction—oops!

private matters

"My boyfriend and I have our anniversary a few days after Christmas. The year we celebrated our first **anniversary**, he gave me one present early on **Christmas Eve**. I wanted to open it in front of my parents. He kept insisting I shouldn't, but I wanted my family to see what a **sweet** guy he was. I was shocked when I opened my gift and saw it was **sexy** lingerie. Guess that's why he didn't want me to open it in front of my parents. . . . "

snack attack

"My family was watching a soccer tournament, and my brother and I were **hungry**. My mom told us not to eat too much because we were going out for dinner later. After I got my **candy** from the concession stand, I saw my brother walking in front of me with a big pile of food on a tray. I **punched** him in the back and jokingly said, 'Fatty! Save some for the rest of us.' Turns out, it wasn't my brother—it was a **stranger**! I felt so bad."

wedding brawls

" My family and I were at a wedding when I had to go to the bathroom really badly. The **ceremony** hadn't started yet, so my mom told me to hurry up and go. I ran out to the hall and **pushed** open the bathroom door, which was pretty heavy. Little did I know, the bride was just on the other side, getting ready to come out. I swung the door **right** into her face! The force of the blow gave her a bloody nose, and we both started crying! **"**

what a scene

" I went to the movies with my boyfriend, and we started making out. **Suddenly** I felt a hard **tap** on my shoulder. I turned around and saw *his mom* staring at me We had no idea she was at the movies too, let alone one row behind us I **apologized** and then ran out of the theater, totally embarrassed. "

very personal shopper

"I was at the **mall** with my boyfriend, and we wandered into Victoria's Secret. I was looking at thongs and found this really sexy hot pink one. I turned around without looking and **jokingly** said to my boyfriend, 'Hey, you should wear this.' Then I noticed it *wasn't* my boyfriend behind me—it was my **grandfather**, who had come to pick me up! I wanted to die. My friends won't let me forget about that incident!"

fire and brimstone

"One Sunday I had to carry one of four 'praise banners' that are mounted on the altar at church. Before the service, I was supposed to take a **flag** from the sanctuary to the back room. As I was carrying it, I didn't notice the huge **candle** beside me, and my banner brushed up against it, catching fire! Everyone was trying to blow out the **flames** while the fire alarm went off. The entire service was **delayed** because of me."

foreign exchange

" I was at Disneyland with my family, and I was hanging out with my cousin, who is fluent in **Spanish**, like me. I saw a large woman on a ride in front of us and said, '*Mira, esa señora apenas cabe en la montaña rusa.*' ('Look, that woman can't fit on the roller coaster.') Then the lady turned around and started to **yell** at me about what I said—in *Spanish*! **Now** I think twice about making rude comments in *any* language. "

urine luck

"My cousins were in town, and after **dinner**, we were just sitting in the car talking. My 3-year-old brother had to go to the **restroom**, so I said I'd take him. We went back in the restaurant, and I decided on the men's room and walked in with him. A **cute** older guy came in, and I figured he'd go into a stall since I was standing there—but he just started peeing in a urinal **right** next to me! I was so horrified!"

about to dye

"As I was going into the shower, I noticed my arms were **purple**. I yelled for help, and my family rushed me to the **hospital**. All of the doctors were puzzled because my skin was this weird color and my breathing was difficult, but all of my other vital signs were normal. Then a **nurse** rubbed my arm with a wet cotton ball. The purple came right off! The shirt I wore earlier that day had **dyed** my skin. As for my breathing—I was having a panic attack!"

bright idea

"
I was at Home Depot with my dad looking at hollow glass **lampshades**. They were the size of a grapefruit, with a hole on one end for the lightbulb. He asked me to **hold** one of them, and somehow I got my hand **stuck** in the hole! After I tried for about five minutes to get free, my dad called over one of the cashiers (who was really **cute**) to help me get my hand out. We didn't want to break the glass, so the cute guy put soap around my wrist. Horrible!
"

check, please

" My crush and I went out to eat with our families— we're all really close. I was wearing a short skirt and kept getting up to get more food at the **buffet** just so he would notice me. One time when I got up, I thought I saw him checking me out. I wanted to make sure I was walking **perfectly**. While concentrating, I walked right into a waiter who was carrying drinks. My clothesand hair were **soaked**! Everyone at the table— including my crush—was cracking up! It was awful. "

flip out

"Every Christmas our **entire** extended family gets together and has a huge party. During the festivities we have a pretty **competitive** talent show, and I really wanted to win last year. My act was a dance, so to make an impression, I did this **amazingly** hard leap called a switch leap. Midair, I farted (so **loud**!) in front of this humongous crowd. I was mortified, and my family still calls me *Tootie*."

wrong note

"My aunt gave me clothes as a Christmas present, and I was totally **grateful**. I wrote her a really thoughtful thank-you note. After I gave it to her, she pulled me aside and gave me a weird **lecture** about being respectful! I couldn't understand why; I'd thought my nice **letter** was very genuine. Then I found out what she was talking about: In my note to her, I'd **written** 'Thank you for the shirt'—only I'd forgotten the *r* in *shirt*. I felt so bad."

cheesy question

" I was out to breakfast with my family and was *dying* for an omelet, so when our really hot waiter came by the table, I asked for the '**choice** of cheese omelet.' He asked what type of cheese I wanted. I had no **idea** what he was talking about, so I just said again, 'I want the choice of cheese.' He **laughed** and went, 'No, do you want American, cheddar, or Swiss?' I felt like an idiot. "

speed bump

"My mom and I were driving when I saw a really hot guy in a blue sports car checking me out. I started **flirting** back, so to show off he sped up and pulled in front of us. He completely cut us off, so my mom started **freaking** out and cussing at him! She even pulled up next to his car and flipped him off! He looked at us like we were **crazy** and just sped away. Then she told me I should **never** date a 'jackass' like him. Horrible!"

family

pass out

"We were at my uncle's house, and his friend, a NFL **quarterback**, was there. We started a game of touch **football**, and I wanted the quarterback to think, Wow, this kid is pretty good! I ran about 30 feet away and turned around to catch one of his passes—just in time to be hit by the ball, *below the belt*! I **dropped** to the ground and blacked out. When I woke up, everyone was standing around me and I was **crying**. To this day, I avoid my uncle's house as much as possible."

wrestle mania

"This guy I was really into asked me to go to a movie with him and his friends. Everything went fine— **until** my dad came to pick us up. My father asked one of the guys if he was a **wrestler**, then my dad looked at me and said, 'She wrestles!' He put me in a **headlock** and gave me a noogie in front of all three guys— including my crush. I was *totally* mortified!"

pop stop

"My boyfriend and I went out with another couple on a double date. On the way to my house, the two of us were making out in the **backseat**. The entire way home, there was this car tailing us *really* closely. It was so **annoying**. But when we pulled into my driveway, we realized it was my *dad* in that car! He'd been watching us go at it the **entire** time!"

guessing game

"My aunt gave me a birthday gift—but when I opened it, I had no clue **what** it was. I held it up anyway and **gushed**, 'It's *so* cute!' My aunt said, 'Well, it's upside down.' I felt **really** bad! But I wish she'd said more— I *still* don't know what it is!"

oh, brother!

"I was shopping with my little brother, who had been obsessed with **scaring** me all day. After I was done shopping, I noticed this **little** figure behind me and recognized my brother's shirt. I wanted to scare him first, so I turned around really fast and made a **crazy** noise—but it wasn't him! It was this little old lady who screamed so **loud**, the whole store stopped and stared. I **apologized**, explaining that I thought she was my brother. My brother was **rolling** on the floor laughing. He saw the whole thing."

shaken up

"Last year my mom and I went on a trip to Ireland. When I got on the plane, the flight attendant stuck his hand out to me. Being **polite**, I shook it. He kind of gave me a surprised look and said, 'Well, thank you!' At first I was **confused** because I thought he had *wanted* me to shake his hand, but then I **realized** he had his hand out just to take my ticket and direct me to my seat."

double talk

“ One day I was **swimming** in my pool with my best friend, my crush, and his twin brother. My little **sister** came outside for a few minutes and asked the two boys, 'So which one of you is which?' My **crush** just goes, '*I'm* the one she likes.' I was totally horrified! **”**

crash 'n' burn

"We were celebrating Christmas at my house, and my little cousin was **playing** around the tree. As I bent down to pick up an ornament that had fallen, he thought it would be funny if he fake-pushed the **tree** toward me. But the tree actually came *down*—breaking all the ornaments! The worst part about it? My brother took a **picture** of the mess, and it became our Christmas card the next year! It was horrible."

family

parent trap

"I was meeting my girlfriend's family for the **first** time, so I really wanted to impress them. When I finally arrived at her house, an older man opened the door. I **immediately** introduced myself and asked, 'Are you her mom's dad or her father's dad?' He was neither—he was my *girlfriend's* dad. Definitely **not** the best first impression!"

light my fire

"

During the holidays last year, I joined my aunt and uncle for Christmas mass. We lit **candles** and were singing when my 3-year-old cousin fell down from his seat. I thought he was hurt, so I **quickly** ducked down to check on him. When I stood up, I smelled something **awful** and realized I had set my hair on fire! I started panicking and smacking my head. The fire **did** die out—but the smell didn't For the rest of the service, the church smelled like burned hair I was so unbelievably uncomfortable.

"

mistle toe

"Last year my family traveled to Paris for Christmas and my parents took us to watch a ballet. I looked really **cute** in my little black dress, so when a **French** guy started talking to me, I smiled, nodded, and **flirted** right back at him—even though I don't speak much French. Then my sister, who is **fluent**, came up and said he was only trying to explain that I was **standing** on his coat! I seriously wanted to die right there!"

nosy neighbor

" I was outside of my grandma's condo with my sister. It was after dinner, and I had really bad gas. I let one rip and it was just **unbelievably** gross—and then I heard footsteps coming around the corner. It was my grandma's **neighbor**, Althea, who is, like, 70. As she went by us, she took a really deep breath in, and said, 'I like that perfume'—and she was being serious. It **reeked** like rotten eggs! My sister and I could barely breathe we were laughing so hard. "

lip service

"It was raining, so my mom gave me a ride to school. As I walked to class, I realized I was getting some **weird** looks from people I didn't even know. It wasn't until I went to the bathroom right before homeroom that I **realized** what was up. When I looked in the mirror, I saw my mom had left a big burgundy lipstick mark right on my **forehead**! I was beyond embarrassed!"

family

roadside attraction

"So the guy I like is walking with me and my friends to get some pizza, when a car pulls up. I couldn't **see** who was in the car, but my guy starts talking and **laughing** with the driver. I got a little jealous, so to be funny, I yell to him, 'Justin, who are you flirting with **now**?' Right then, my crush turns around and yells back, 'My **dad**!' I was horrified!"

in the cards

"This guy asked me to go with him to homecoming this past fall, and I said yes, not thinking it was a big deal. We went with a whole group of friends and had fun, but nothing happened between us—we stayed friends. Months later, we started getting Christmas cards in the mail, including that guy's parents. They used our homecoming picture as the cover of the holiday card they sent to everyone! He wasn't even my boyfriend! My parents won't let me live it down."

family

off her rocker

" I'm in a band and we had this great gig where all our friends and families came to support us. Everybody was **really** into the music and a couple of guys started a mosh pit. My Aunt Mimi noticed the guys moshing and **freaked** out. She went running toward the pit, waving her arms and yelling, 'Break it up, boys! Stop fighting!' **Everybody** started laughing. I just kept **playing**, hoping nobody knew she was my aunt! "

sight unseen

"I was with my boyfriend and his family watching that Ray Charles **movie**. I was a little bored and not paying too much attention to the story. After it was over, my boyfriend's father mentioned that he had passed away before the movie was even released. I said, 'That's so **sad** he never got to watch the movie they made about his life.' The whole family looked at each other **strangely**, and my boyfriend said, 'Uh, he was blind.'"

mr. wrong

"My sister and I were out shopping when I saw a really cute guy. I could only see the back of him, but he had a **nice** body and I liked his shirt. To get him to notice me, I said, 'Look at that cute guy!' But when he turned around, he was **old** and had a huge beard! My sister nearly peed herself **laughing**!"

royal flush

"Right before my family and I went rafting, I had to go to the bathroom and I couldn't find the **flusher** in the Port-A-Potty anywhere. After about five minutes, I gave up because we were **running** late. The lady who went in after me said, 'That's kinda gross.' Then her husband—in front of **everyone** else there—said, 'So you haven't learned to flush the toilet yet?' To make matters **worse**, the couple turned out to be going on the rafting trip with us!"

hunger pains

" My parents, my sister, and I had been shopping all day. I was exhausted and starving when we finally went to HomeTown Buffet for dinner. I went through all the food lines, but I wasn't seeing many things I could eat as a vegetarian. I noticed five **more** food-cart things across the room and headed toward them, and **slammed** into a huge, wall-sized mirror! The food carts I'd seen were just a reflection of the ones I'd already looked at. So, I was in pain, hungry, and practically **everyone** in the whole restaurant was staring at me. It was awful. "

"I laughed so hard that I peed my pants!"
see page 127

friends

It's so **true** what they always say:
humiliation loves **company**.

say cheese

"
My friend and I were at a party when she saw her **crush**. She wanted to go talk to him, but couldn't because she had to leave right away. She was really **bummed**, so I decided to **sneak** a picture on my phone and send it to her to cheer her up. I was trying to be discreet, but when I took the picture, the **flash** went off! All his friends gave me weird looks. Her crush was like, 'Um, who are you taking a picture of?' I was mortified!
"

the real feel

"One day my friends an I were walking through a department store at the mall. I spotted a male mannequin wearing this shirt that looked so soft, I just had to touch it! As I started feeling it, the mannequin moved! Turns out it was a real live man who was just standing really still. He gave me a weird look, and I quickly apologized and ran away as fast as I could. Oops!"

ballbuster

"A group of my friends went to the mini-golf course one weekend. I'm pretty bad at the game, so my crush was giving me a few pointers and putting his arms around me to help me swing. After the lesson, I closed my eyes and swung hard, hoping that the ball wouldn't land in the water. As I was swinging, I hit something behind me and heard my crush yell out. I turned around and saw that I had smacked him right in the crotch with my golf club. Oops!"

friends

adult content

"Last summer my friend invited me to visit Las Vegas with her family. One night she and I decided to go out on our own. As we were about to drive away, I **remembered** that I had left my hair straightener on in the master bathroom, which was off the room where my friend's **parents** were staying. I ran back in to turn it off. But when I barged in, I caught her parents having sex! We just **stared** at each other in shock. I wished I'd stayed at home!"

girls on film

"My friend and I went to a theme park and got in line for a rollercoaster. As we stepped into our car, we noticed a super-cute guy sitting in front of us. So throughout the whole ride we made kissy faces and hand gestures behind him. Afterward we headed down the exit ramp, and the guy was standing there laughing. My friend and I looked behind him and saw a huge screen showing a digital picture taken of us during the ride! We were totally caught."

mistaken identity

" My friend and I were at a birthday party for one of her relatives. I decided to join in on a **conversation**, so I walked up to one of the adults and made small talk. I remarked, 'Wow, you look really great for being Shirley's grandmother!' She **stared** at me and then said, 'I'm her aunt.' Ouch! I apologized and **avoided** her the rest of the night. "

urine trouble

In eighth grade we had these little scooters in our gym class. One day my friend was pushing me on a scooter, and we were going so **fast** that we couldn't stop. I went flying into the wall, and I **laughed** so hard I peed my pants! And if that wasn't embarrassing enough, my friend had to tell the teacher—who happened to be my crush's mom—so that I could change my clothes. People were talking about it for **weeks**.

photo madness

"

I was at a friend's Sweet Sixteen party last year, and she hired a professional photographer to take random pictures of us. I had a really bad cold and had been blowing my nose a lot. Later on at the party, the photographer played a slide show of the pictures, and up popped a big photo of me with a *huge* booger on my face! I was so embarrassed.

"

friends

just snot right

"We were playing Spin the Bottle, even though I was coming down with something and my nose was really stuffy. This guy **spun**, and it landed on me! I felt awkward with my eyes closed, so I opened them, and the first thing I saw was my best friend standing over us **watching**. I started to laugh, but because my lips were pressed against his, it came out like a snort—and snot shot out of my nose. It was all over both of our faces! I was **mortified**."

shakin' it up

"I was at my friend's house along with her boyfriend and a really cute friend of his. The four of us were hanging out, and her boyfriend thought it would be funny to see which girl could shake her butt better—my friend or me. I said that I'd go first, so I started to shake it—but in the middle of my moves, I farted really loud. They all fell to the ground laughing. It was so awful that I wanted to die!"

friends

off campus

" My friends and I wanted to have some fun, so we crashed a frat **party**. At first we blended in. But then this one guy asked me what classes I was taking. I didn't want him to know I was in high school, so I said, 'The **main** classes.' He was like, 'What?' I had no idea what courses college students take, so I finally **admitted** my real age. After that, they kicked us out of the party! To this day everyone loves to remind me of that awful night. **"**

bad santa

"One Christmas I was out for coffee with my crush and friends. My crush dared me to sit on Santa's lap and ask for a date. I wanted to **impress** him, so I climbed onto Santa's lap and said, 'Santa, all I want for Christmas is a **date**!' Suddenly Santa said my name. I pulled off his **beard** and saw it was my science teacher! Even worse, my friends ran away laughing and left me **sitting** on his lap—*and* I had to spend the rest of the year in his class!"

boogeyman

"

I was hanging out with my friends when my crush, who is also a friend, sat next to me. He began **flirting** with me and held my hand—I was so excited! Then he started talking about how he hates it when people have boogers hanging out of their noses and they don't **notice** it. He turned to me and started laughed again. When I asked why, he moved both of our hands up to my face and said, 'Get that booger. I don't want to touch it.' I was *mortified*!

"

treasure hunt

"One day at lunch I set my retainers down on my tray before I began eating. After I had finished, I automatically dumped my tray in the trash can. Then it hit me: My $350 retainers! My friends and I took the trash cans outside, the staff gave us gloves, and we started digging through two nasty piles of garbage. Half an hour later my friend offered me a piece of gum. That was when I realized that my retainers had been in my mouth the entire time!"

wrong solution

"I went to a tanning salon for the **first** time, and I came out with little red bumps all over my body. They burned really, really badly, so I went up to the guy at the counter and **complained** that one of the tanning beds burned me. Turns out it wasn't the bed: The 'tanning oil' I had used was **actually** cleaning solution for the tanning beds, and it irritated my skin. I was so **embarrassed**. Now I always make sure to read labels!"

friends

showering off

" I was in France on vacation waiting for a train. The **toilets** at the station were high-tech: You put money in to open them, and they clean **automatically**. Unfortunately the instructions were in French, so I couldn't figure out what to do! I stuck my head out to ask my friends, and when I shut the door again, the **lights** went out and jet showers began **spraying** disinfectant. I started screaming while my friends tried to open the door! "

body talk

"In my youth Bible group, our pastor asked us, 'What is the most sexual part of your body?' I **immediately** raised my hand and yelled, 'Vagina!' He **frowned** and said, 'That's not the answer.' Another kid raised his hand and said, 'Your brain!' Our pastor said he was correct—then **everyone** turned around to look at me! I felt *so* embarrassed."

friends

locked out

"My friend was totally crushing on this guy, and she wanted to know where his locker was so she could go there and flirt with him. To find out, we **followed** him one morning. When he stopped to talk, we bolted for the first locker we saw and **pretended** that my friend was having trouble opening her locker. Next thing we knew, he was *right* behind us asking, 'Why are you trying to open my locker?' We were *so* busted. All we could say was, 'Oops,' and walk away!"

facedown

"Last year my college gave the female students a goody bag of feminine products with items like deodorant and face wash. I got so **excited** when I saw what I thought was a Wet-Nap—I love using them at restaurants. I quickly took it out of the package and wiped it **all** over my face. My roommate saw what I was doing and started laughing **hysterically**. When she finally composed herself, she said, 'Those are *personal* cleansing cloths—they're *not* for your face.' It's still my **most** humiliating experience ever!"

wet and wild

"I was in the pool at my friend's house, and I *really* had to go to the bathroom, but we were having so much fun. All of a sudden it became harder to hold it. I ran over to the sliding door and tried to open it, but it wouldn't budge. My friend's mom opened it for me, but it was too late. I peed *right* in front of her! I said, 'Sorry, I'm really wet from the pool.' She just looked at me—I could tell she knew what I'd done!"

duffel shuffle

"

I work at a tennis game booth during the summer. One day my friend carried my duffel **bag** to the booth. Once I got there, I opened it, and the first thing I saw was a bra. I figured my friend was playing a **joke** on me, so I took out the bra and put it on over my shirt and started **juggling** some tampons that were there too. When I was done, the girl who worked in the booth right across from us asked, 'What are you doing with my stuff?'

"

144

present tense

"My best friend's mom bought me this cheesy jewelry box as a Hanukkah gift. She told me I would **love** it, but my friend said it was just embarrassing. When I opened it, I immediately called my friend on her private number. When the line picked up, I started **blabbing** on and on about how much I hated the gift. Then her **mom** says, 'Sam's at her father's house, but I can call and give her the message if you want.' I hung up and stayed away from my friend's house for a long, **long**, time."

santa pause

" It has become a tradition each Christmas for my friends and me to get together and take **pictures** with Santa Claus. We were sitting on his knee when I realized that I had to fart. I tried **really** hard to hold it in, but I couldn't. So I figured if it passed quietly, I would be fine. When it came out, I felt relieved—it was **silent**. That's when Santa politely turned to me and said, 'Excuse *you*!'—he felt the **heat**! Everyone burst out laughing! It was totally embarrassing! "

drowned out

"I was on the phone with my best friend when nature called. So midsentence, I went to answer nature while we kept talking. But then as I was pulling up my pants, I **dropped** the phone into the toilet! I got the phone out by the **antenna**, but it was dead. When I called her back on our other phone, she was like, 'I heard a **splash**: What happened?' To have to explain that— even to your best friend—is embarrassing!"

handy snacks

" My friends and I were at the movies waitin for the movie to start. My best guy friend was sitting next to me, and he had a **popcorn** bag in his lap. We were both munching on it. When I went to put my hand in the bag to get **more**, the bag wasn't there—and I ended up grabbing at his *crotch*! He had handed the bag over to someone **else** to hold. Later that night we both laughed about it, but right then, **seriously**, I could have died! "

park place

"I was driving with my friend to school. We were **almost** there—we just had to turn right and find a parking spot. So I got into the turning lane and **waited** for the line to start moving, but after waiting for forever, my friend suddenly burst into **laughter**. She was laughing so hard that she couldn't even stop to tell me what was so funny. **Finally**, when she caught her breath, she mumbled, 'Hillary, you're behind a line of **parked** cars.' I had pulled into a parking lane!"

total relaxation

"I was at a spa-like camp, and my friend and I had signed up for yoga classes in the morning. It was nice until they told us to hold this weird pose for a long time. I started to get uncomfortable, so I decided to shift my weight around—and I farted really loudly! Someone in the back of the class said, 'Let the gases flow.' My friend started laughing, and soon the whole class joined her."

friends

half-baked

" All of my friends were returning from really **great** Spring break vacations. I decided to try out some self-tanner and **pretend** that I'd gone away somewhere fun too. So one girl asked me where I'd gone, and I **immediately** told her I'd been in Cancún. She said, 'Then why don't you have a **real** tan?' I looked down at my palms and realized they were orange and streaky. Everyone **knew** my vacation was a total fraud. "

potty talk

"I was in the restroom at Ryan's, this restaurant my parents like to go to. As I washed my hands, a lady behind me said hi. I figured she was just **nice**, so I said hi back. She asked, 'How are you?' and I said, 'Fine.' Then she asked, 'How are your kids?' I thought, Huh? I don't have any!—until I turned and saw her . . . on her cell **phone**! I felt so stupid!"

friends

out of shape

"My parents placed an ad in the paper for this pool table we wanted to sell. This one lady called, and I was just about to pass the phone over to my mom, when the lady asked, 'What's its shape?' I thought it was a pretty **weird** question for her to ask, and I said, 'Um, it's just a rectangle.' The lady started laughing and said, 'No, I mean what **condition** is it in?' I was so totally embarrassed, I just handed the phone to my mom without saying another word!"

face-off

"My friends and I were on our way home from the movies when we stopped off at Wendy's. When we went back in the car, my crush told me I had something on my face. He tried to wipe it off, but it wouldn't come off. When I realized what he was doing, I told him I didn't think it was going to come off. Of course he asked why, and I had to reply, 'Uh, because it's a zit!' Of course, the whole car started laughing at me!"

jet fuel

" I invited my best friend and two hot guys to come hang out in the Jacuzzi at my house. While the jets were still running, I thought it would be **safe** to let out a fart, because the bubbles would look like they came from the Jacuzzi. Little did I know, my friend had **just** turned off the jets. To my horror she asked, 'Why are the jets still running?' The only **bubbles** were the ones coming out of me! The guys started **laughing**, and I was mortified. "

friends

special delivery

" When working on a group project with my crush we got **distracted** and started talking about our summers. I talked about how me and friends ordered Domino's **pizza** a lot and the same ugly pizza guy came **every** time and would always check us out. Then my crush asks what the pizza guy was driving. 'A truck,' I said. Then he asks what **color**, and I said, 'Red.' He said, 'That was my brother!' "

thin ice

"

My synchronized skating team was at practice, and there were some hot hockey guys **watching** up in the stands. Me and one of my teammates were the closest to them, so of course we weren't **focusing** on what our coach was saying! Then, all of a sudden, we heard our coach yell, 'Will you stop looking at those guys on the bleachers and pay **attention**?' We saw the guys laugh, and then leave! I was mortified!

"

friends

curtain call

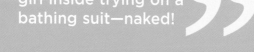

" My friend and I were at the mall trying on clothes for summer. Our fitting rooms were right next to each other, so every time I tried on an **outfit**, I'd open up the curtain to her dressing room and show her. Well, after trying on my last outfit, I opened her **curtain** only to see that she wasn't in there anymore! There was **another** girl inside trying on a bathing suit—naked! "

cake walk

"My friend Stacey **reserved** a party room for her birthday. After we ate and she opened her presents, we all went out to play a few **games**. An hour later I went back to get some cake. I didn't see any of my friends but there were a bunch of Stacey's relatives I didn't **recognize**. I found the cake and wolfed it down. Twenty minutes later, with a good quarter of the cake in my stomach, I noticed the **decorations** read, 'Happy Birthday, Vanessa!' I had just **crashed** some random girl's party!"

"...the toilet paper was on the floor, covered in blood!"

see page 184

school

Nothing like being in **front** of an audience when you just want to **evaporate**.

a star is born

"Around the holidays my school always decorates a huge tree in the entryway. Last year I volunteered to **decorate** because I knew my crush was decorating as well. When the teacher asked for **someone** to climb a ladder and place ornaments at the top. I climbed the ladder smiling as **bright** as the star I was placing. But I must have been too busy looking at my crush—I leaned too far into the tree and made it **fall** over. It was horrible!"

lady in red

"I was thrilled when I was cast as Lady Capulet in *Romeo and Juliet*. I had never been **onstage**, so the night of the first performance, I freaked out. To make matters worse, I had my period. I pulled myself together but broke down afterward. I started talking to my friend about how horrible I'd done and how it was because I felt so **gross** because of my period. Then, I heard a roar of laughter from the audience. My **microphone** was on—the tech crew hadn't turned it off!"

school

dog run

"I was walking to my bus stop and saw this angry-looking poodle. I am *terrified* of dogs—even poodles! The next thing I knew, he was **chasing** me down the street! I was screaming my head off. Later on, I logged onto MySpace, and there was a message titled, 'DaShaun's Wild Run!' I clicked on it and saw a **video** of myself running from the poodle. Someone from my bus stop recorded it on a camera phone and posted it **online**. Everyone saw it. Horrible!"

love hurts

"I was sitting with my best friend one day, and she was really bummed because she had just broken up with her boyfriend. I was trying to **cheer** her up, so I told her, 'I love you this much.' As I said it, I spread my arms **wide** to show her just how much—and ended up **smacking** someone on the butt. I turned around and saw it was the principal! He gave me an **evil** look. I wanted to die, but at least it got my friend laughing again!"

jersey error

" Every year my school has a huge football game against our rival. Some girls had the players' jersey numbers **painted** on their faces, so I decided to draw my friend's number on my face. Later on, my friend asked me why I had the letter p written on my face. I had accidentally reversed the number 9 in the **mirror**! It was like that the whole game. "

wind breaker

"

I was waiting at the bus stop and had my iPod cranked up really **loud**. I was feeling pretty gassy, and I sensed a fart coming. It felt like a quiet one, so I just let it **out**. But when everyone at my stop **suddenly** looked over at me, I knew it was loud. I was horrified!

"

breakthrough role

"My volleyball team was asked to participate as extras in a TV movie. We were supposed to play a game in the **background** while the main characters were talking. I was really **excited** about the opportunity to be on camera, so I tried my best to play well. The ball came **flying** toward me, and I hit it to another player. But instead it veered a little off-center—and hit the **cameraman** right in the head! Needless to say, I warmed the bench for the rest of the shoot."

multitasker

" I was in the middle of taking a test, and it was dead **quiet** in the room. I really had to **sneeze** but was trying so hard to keep it in. Finally I couldn't hold back anymore, and I let it out—but at the end of my sneeze, I farted really **loud**! *Everyone* heard it. Now my new nickname is Snarty (*sneeze* and *fart* mixed together). Horrible! "

french kiss

"My teacher prefers that we e-mail him our essays. I successfully uploaded my paper on the French Revolution one day, and I was **relieved** it had gone through—usually I'm pretty bad with computers. But then he e-mailed me back asking, 'What does your bikini have to do with the French Revolution?' I was **confused** until I realized that I had accidentally attached the **wrong** file—a picture of me in a swimsuit, blowing a kiss to the camera! It was so embarrassing."

school

butt double

"My best guy friend and I have this **joke** where we'll sneak up and pinch each other. One day between classes I saw him in the **hall**. So I crept up behind him and pinched his butt pretty hard. He **jumped** and turned around, but then I realized it wasn't my friend—it was my history **teacher**! He looked at me like I was crazy."

anatomy 101

"In science class we did a lab that other students videotaped—so we could **learn** by watching it over again. After we were done, they played the **video** for our class. When my part came up, the camera just **zoomed** in on my chest for an entire minute! Apparently the cameraman thought *that* was more interesting than the project. I was so annoyed!"

noisemaker

"

I was sitting in class when all of a sudden, I got these **intense** stomach pains. I knew that I would need to use the bathroom very soon, but my teacher was in the **middle** of a lecture and the class was taking notes quietly. I thought that I could **silently** let out just a tiny bit of gas to make my stomach feel a little better. I was shocked by how **loud** it came out! I was so embarrassed that everyone heard it— I wanted to die.

"

swing state

" One time in school I was carrying my bag, and it was really **heavy**. I decided to swing it really fast so it would go over my shoulder. I whipped it around my back— and when I looked up again, I saw my **principal** crouched down in pain behind me. That was when I realized I had hit him with my bag— in his crotch! He limped away as my face turned bright red. Now he never makes eye contact! "

passed up

" I was sitting in class right next to my guy friend. He passed me a **note** and whispered something I couldn't hear. When I opened it, it was a long letter about his **secret** feelings for me! I was so psyched, I **immediately** whispered that I had feelings for him too. He gave me a weird look and said, 'I *said* that was for Kayla'—the girl sitting *next* to me. I was **supposed** to pass it to *her*! All I could do was sink down in my seat, completely humiliated. "

hands down

"

I really wanted my crush to know I liked him, so I wrote him a **note** that said, 'Hey, it's Kari. I really like you, and I've liked you since the beginning of the year. Do you want to hang out sometime?' As I placed my note on his desk, the girl who was collecting our **homework** added it to the pile and gave it to the **teacher**—with my note on top. I watched in **horror** as he read it. My teacher looked my way and simply raised an eyebrow. Humiliation!

"

seat warmer

"One day at a football game, I saw my crush. I thought that he was waving **me** over, and since some of my friends were nearby, I went to sit next to him. When I sat down, he was like, 'Um . . . I was kind of saving that seat.' I just **laughed** and said, 'Okay, whatever,' because we always **joke** like that together. But then two seconds later, his **girlfriend** came over to me and said, 'You're in my seat—can you scoot over?' It was *definitely* awkward."

dramatic scene

"I wanted to make this guy I really liked notice me. When my friends asked me to **perform** a dance routine with them at the school talent show, I decided this would be my chance. When I got onstage, I was concentrating so hard on not messing up that I didn't notice how close I was to the **edge**. During the part of the dance where we were all supposed to slide to one side, I flew right off the stage! The whole audience **gasped**. I got his attention after all!"

gym period

"I had just gotten my period, so before I headed to gym class, I put a layer of toilet paper in my underwear to make sure it didn't leak onto my **shorts**. We were playing volleyball and I got really into the game. All of a sudden **everyone**—including my ex and his friends—started staring at me and **laughing**. I looked down and the toilet paper was on the floor, covered in blood! I just about *died*."

baby mama

"During a school-band concert, my friends and I were trashing this girl Lisa who was **performing** with the band. We were saying stuff like, 'She never stops crying,' and 'She looks like a baby with those pigtails.' At the end of the show, the people in front of us started clapping loudly and **yelling**, 'Yeah, you go, Lisa!' When I looked closer I recognized Lisa's **parents**! Her mom was in the same pigtails Lisa wore every day. I felt so bad."

school

floor manager

"During my freshman year managing basketball, I was keeping score at a scrimmage. At one point during the game, the boys went into a huddle. The ball started **bouncing** to me, so I went to grab it—not realizing the **cord** of the scoring machine was wrapped around my foot. As I got up, I **tripped** on the cord and fell flat on my face. All the guys let out this loud *ooooh* sound, but none of them even got up to try to help me. It was the worst."

cream of weep

"In my art class we were making collages about ourselves with pictures from **magazines**. When I heard some of my classmates **laughing**, I looked up and saw them holding a picture of a smiley face drawn with cream. I thought the picture would be great for my **collage**, so I shouted across the room, 'Oh—I need that!' Everyone started **laughing**, and I couldn't understand why. Later someone told me that the smiley-face picture was an ad for feminine-itch cream!"

school

full moon

" I went into a bathroom stall at my school and **locked** the door. As usual, I went to go cover the seat with paper, and pulled down my pants and undies. But when I **turned** to sit on the toilet, I realized the door hadn't locked! It **swung** open the other way—so I was mooning this girl washing her hands. She couldn't stop laughing! "

speech therapy

"Everyone had written essays for drug-prevention week, and I had to read mine at an **assembly**. My best friend Carly played a practical joke on me and switched my **essay** with another paper for our sex-education class. I got up to read it and—without realizing it—started my speech with, 'Abstinence has its benefits.' The entire audience started **laughing**, and then the teachers started lecturing me in front of everyone about how inappropriate it was!"

scene and heard

"I was **starring** in a play at school—and half the town was there for opening night. I messed up my lines a couple of times and was really **upset** about it. So when I walked off the stage after my **final** scene, I told my friend, 'I messed up four f***ing times! Can you believe it?!' Make that *five* times—after the show, my other friend told me that I hadn't turned off my **microphone** and the *whole audience* had heard me. I was so completely embarrassed!"

pepped up

"I was at a school pep rally and wanted to tell my crush, who is a football player, that I liked him. My **friends** and I planned to yell, 'We love you, Jamall!' after his name was announced during the event. They called his name, and I **screamed** it, but my friends totally chickened out. It was just *me* yelling—and of course he heard it! But some good came out of it—we've been **dating** ever since!"

language lesson

"There was this **new** kid in my school who was really cute. One of my friends told me that he was a **foreign** exchange student. I decided to introduce myself, so I went up to him and asked very loudly and slowly, 'What . . . country . . . are . . . you . . . from?' He paused and looked at me, then said, 'Uh, the United States.' He wasn't from another country at all—he had transferred from a school across the **state**!"

art lover

66 I was on break during play rehearsal when I saw Cyndi, a girl on the stage crew I had a thing for, painting the **background** for the set. I sat down next to her—but when I looked up, all I saw was her **horrified** expression! I was sitting on the scenery she had just finished **painting**. Not only did I ruin her work, but I also had a **huge** paint stain on my butt—and I didn't get the girl. 99

class jean-ius

"My friends and I were in class and our teacher was talking, but we weren't listening. We were **reading** my copy of *Seventeen*, and my friend kept tapping me on the shoulder and saying, 'That would look cute with . . . ' So when I felt **another** tap on my shoulder, I said, 'That would look cute with those jeans you gave me for my birthday.' My **teacher** said, 'When did I give you those?' He was standing behind me, watching me read! Oops . . ."

miss spoken

"I was in Spanish class and our teacher announced that he wanted to see all the **boys** after class. I tried to tell him, in Spanish, that he was being sexist by ignoring the girls. Instead it came out as, 'You are sexually **ignoring** the girls.' Everyone cracked up, including our Spanish teacher, who almost **fell** off his chair because he was laughing so hard."

stage wrong

"

I missed the **tryouts** for my school play, so I got stuck working stage crew. My job was to raise and lower the curtains, which I'd done before, so I didn't really pay **attention** when I was shown how to do it. During the second night's performance, I **totally** grabbed the wrong lever and made the curtain fall **right** on four kids on stage! On top of that, everyone was yelling my name, so the audience knew it was my fault. I'll never work stage crew again!

"

book drive

"I was walking back to my car after school when my crush made his way toward me. I threw my books on top of my car so we could **talk**. When we were done I got in my car to go home. Before I got very far, though, I heard a big **thump**. My books had fallen **all** over the road. Not only was I **embarrassed** to be picking up my schoolbooks from the street—but my crush was **right** there in his car and saw everything. I was horrified!"

school

in a bind

" When my English teacher passed out some papers for us to read that night as homework, I **opened** my binder and put the paper in the rings. I leaned over my binder to **snap** the rings shut, but when I did, the rings clipped me right on my chest. I guess I winced and shrieked kind of loudly from the pain and that made **everyone** look over at me. When they realized what was happening, they all started laughing I wanted to shrivel up and die! "

pop quiz

"I was **bored** in class, so I decided to play around with the zit on my face. I thought everything was fine until the guy sitting next to me **looked** over and said, 'Dude, what is on your *face*?' Turns out I had popped a pimple, and it was bleeding! That's a **hard** one to live down."

best in show

" I was at this athletic-awards ceremony at my school, and when they got to Most Improved Athlete, I was **sure** it would be me. I was totally **ready** for this moment, so I stood up to go get the award before they even called my name—but then when they announced who had won, it **wasn't** me! I didn't know what to do, so I just pretended I'd gotten up to fix my skirt. It was beyond humiliating! "

bare essentials

"I was about to go on a school trip to Costa Rica. At an informational meeting, our teacher told us it would be a good idea to bring **thongs**—I couldn't believe it! Why would our teacher say we needed thongs? My confusion must have showed, because one of the other teachers looked **right** at me and said, 'You do know she means thong **sandals**, right?' Everyone started laughing— it was so hilarious!"

heart attack

" It was the last day of school, and I really wanted my crush to sign my yearbook—but because he wasn't in any of my classes, I asked my friend, who was in his English class, to take it over. When she *finally* came back with his signature, I was ecstatic—that is, until she told me what happened! He didn't recognize my name, so he looked up my picture to see who I was, and **saw** his picture—where I had drawn a **huge** red heart around his face! "

205

"I jumped up to catch the ball—and my pants fell to my ankles, exposing my granny panties..."

see page 212

fashion

Even the **best-dressed** intentions can have **humiliating** consequences.

heel no

"While I visited my grandparents in the **country**, I went to buy some groceries. Thinking there might be some hot guys, I put on my favorite **stilettos**. When I got there this cute marine **smiled** at me. I smiled back, winked, and my heel got caught in a crack in the pavement and I hit the ground. I was absolutely **mortified** as the marine came over and said, 'You've got to be from the city—any country girl would know not to wear those heels!'"

hot flash

"I went on vacation with my best friend and her family to Florida. One day all of us headed to the **pool** at the resort where we were staying, and my best friend, her mom, her dad, and I were lying out **together**. When I got out of my chair and bent down to get a magazine, the top of my bathing suit **snapped** open—and my best friend's dad got a full view of my boobs!"

bus wrecked

"One morning on the bus to go to school, I sat sideways with my back to the window and my feet up on the seat. My **crush** got on the bus after me, sat behind me, and started **talking** to me. It was great—until the bus driver stopped so suddenly that I **flew** to the side and smacked my face on the seat in front of me. My crush laughed **loudly** and said, 'Wow, your day is starting off bad. You sat in gum too!'"

sweet cheeks

"I was waiting in line to get a cake at the grocery store. I got **tired** of standing, so I decided to lean on the **cupcake** case. Turns out, there was no glass around the case—and I fell right in! Everyone laughed when they saw my butt covered in **icing**."

fashion

draw a crowd

"I was at softball practice one day, standing in the field, when I noticed the drawstring that held up my **sweatpants** was untied. As I tried to retie it, it broke! I kept playing with the **string**, but then a ball was hit my way. Without thinking, I **jumped** up to catch the ball— and my pants fell to my **ankles**, exposing my granny panties in front of my coach and the *entire* boys' tennis team. I just stood there completely embarrassed and awkward!"

fashion

undressed to impress

" On my best friend's birthday, a bunch of us took her out to a **fancy** restaurant. I wore a cute short red halter-dress tied around my **neck**. It kept riding up, so I kept pulling it down under the table. I tugged a little too hard and all of a sudden the tie came **undone** and the whole top fell down! As I stood up to run to the bathroom, the bottom started riding up **again**! Everyone got a peek. "

bottoms up

"

I brought some friends to my beach house one weekend, and my dad took us out in the boat to go **tubing**. During my turn I hit a **huge** wave out of nowhere and wiped out. As my dad was steering the boat back to get me, I realized my bikini bottoms had come **off**. I couldn't see them anywhere! So I had to have **everyone** turn around as I climbed back on board and wrapped a towel around myself. I was so humiliated.

"

fashion

clothes call

" My best friend and I were shopping at a department store, and I found some great **dresses** to try on. When we got to the fitting room, I saw a few guys standing around. I didn't like the fact that they were in the women's room, so I **demanded** they leave. **Suddenly** the manager came in and told me that I was the one who needed to get out—it was the *men's* dressing room. All the guys were **snickering**, and I ran out of there, mortified! "

he says/she says

"I was at a store and a weird-looking girl commented on a **dress** I was admiring. I told her it would look **great** on her. Then she glared at me and said, 'I'm a guy I was going to buy this for my *girlfriend*.' Oops!"

fashion

double stuff

> I was over at a friend's house, and we went to the beach. I **borrowed** a bathing suit from my friend, and she's bigger than me on top, so I **stuffed** the chest with toilet paper. When we got there, the **cute** lifeguard kept looking over at me, so I smiled at him and made eye contact. He started laughing hysterically, and I didn't know why—until my friend told me my toilet-paper boobs were **sticking** out of the suit for everyone to see! I was *completely* humiliated.

fashion

zip up

" I had my period, and between classes I **ran** to the bathroom to change my pad. While I was in there the **late** bell rang. There wasn't a trash can in my stall, and I couldn't waste more time, so I tucked the used pad in my **backpack** and ran to class. Once I got to my seat, the boy next to me gave me a weird look. I glanced down at my bag and saw that I hadn't **closed** the zipper. My gross pad was in full view! **"**

what a bummer

> It was Spirit Week at my school, and I was a speaker at the **assembly**. As an example of what to wear for **Pajama Day**, I wore a really cute outfit that was yellow with blue moons and stars. As I was walking down to the stage, everyone was **clapping** and cheering. But after the assembly, people told me, 'Nice thong!' and 'Your thong was so cute!' Apparently my pajamas were see-through, and my **whole** school got a clear view of everything underneath!

fashion

excess baggage

" I took my school **backpack** on a weekend trip. When I got back, I dumped my clothes out onto my bed and put my books back in. The next day I went to school, talked to some friends, and walked to biology. I sat down at my desk—and that was when I **noticed** a pair of **underwear** hanging off my bag in plain sight! It had gotten stuck to the Velcro on the bag when I was unpacking from my trip. **Everyone** saw it, and no one told me! "

private performance

> On Saturday mornings I get up early to spend some time by myself. One morning I was **singing** to the mirror, using a hairbrush as a 'microphone.' I was really getting into it, and when I tried to hit a high note, I squeaked pretty **loudly**. When I heard a **snicker** outside my room, I opened my door—completely **forgetting** I was wearing only a bra and short shorts—to find that my older brother and his hot friend were listening the whole time!

fashion

strung out

"When I first started using tampons, I would forget to tuck in the string. One day I was flirting with my crush, acting cute in my new denim **miniskirt**. My friend Beth came up and whispered, 'You've got a **string** hanging from your skirt; I'll get it.' Then I felt this sharp pain 'down under.' My friend **gasped** and my crush laughed. When I looked down, I saw my used tampon on the ground! My friend quickly hauled me away to the girls' bathroom but people were pointing."

poor baby

> We were at the playground, and my little cousin was in a baby **swing**, so I crammed my legs down into the holes in the seat next to him—and I got **stuck**. My older cousin flipped the swing upside down to try to free me, but it didn't work. The only way to get out was to take off my **pants**! I slid out of them while everyone at the nearby pool watched. After I put them back on, I realized there were security cameras **taping** the whole thing.

fashion

northern exposure

"Every year my school has a holiday dance. My favorite song came on, so I ran to the dance floor. My ex-boyfriend's **new** girl was standing right next to me, and I guess she thought it would be **funny** to step on the hem of my strapless floor-length gown and pull it down. It worked even better than she thought—when the **dress** fell down, my bra came off *with* it! Everyone saw, including my ex. It was awful!"

board walk

"I was wearing a new black tank top with a strapless bra to school and got a lot of compliments. I felt **ecstatic**! So when my teacher asked for a volunteer, I raised my hand. I strutted my way to the board and wrote down the **answer**. Before I turned around to face the class, I scootched up my bra. When I sat down, people were **snickering**, but I had no idea why. Then my ex pointed at my shirt—I had white **fingerprints** on my breasts from the chalk!"

fashion

juicy fruit

" On my **first** day of high school, our teacher asked us to say one thing we noticed about the person sitting next to us, so the boy next to me said, 'I noticed she likes **watermelons**.' Everybody was looking around, confused. That was when I realized I had forgotten to put a belt on—and was **exposing** my red watermelon thong to the whole class! I was *mortified*! "

toss-up

"

I was at the mall with my mom having a 'bonding' day. We were in the dressing rooms together, so I threw over all the **clothes** I didn't like so she could try them on. Well, she just threw them back, so I started **laughing** and kept throwing stuff over, thinking that we were having a **fun** clothes fight. But then she threw everything over *again*. Then she **knocked** and asked, 'Are you ready to pay?' It was the dressing-room attendant the whole time! I just paid and **left**, mortified.

"

fashion

intimates moment

"One morning I realized **all** my bras and panties were dirty, so I asked my mom if she could wash them. Later that day I made plans with my **crush** to study together. When we went up to my room, I went into complete **shock**! My mom had my panties spread out on my bed and my bras were hung around my ceiling fan! Our dryer was being **repaired**. My crush started cracking up and said, 'Nice room.' I was **humiliated**.

I never asked my mom to do my laundry again!"

fashion

shoplifter

> I was shopping at the mall and I was running **late** to meet my mother. Right in the middle of trying on a shirt, my mom called to tell me that I had to leave right away or she'd take my cell phone away. I **dashed** from the dressing room and ran out of the store, totally forgetting that I still had the shirt on. The **alarm** went off. I had to go back inside and explain myself to the cute attendant! I'm still too mortified to return to that Hollister store.

slipup

"I was head over heels for this guy, and I knew he would be at my friend's party one night. I wore this cute **dress** that showed all my curves. It was white with red flowers—and I looked hot! When I got to the party and went to the bathroom, I realized that the dress was **totally** see-through—and I was wearing white undies with *big green frogs* on them! **Everyone**, including my crush, saw my Kermit the Frog panties! I pretty much hid in the corner all night."

fashion

rise and shine

" I got a black **dress** covered in sparkles for a party. I knew I'd be **dancing** and I'd get really hot, so I put on a ton of deodorant. So I'm at the **party**, dancing with all these hot guys, and this great song comes on. The DJ yells, 'Raise your hands!' When we do, everyone around me starts **laughing**. I laugh too—until my sister tells me that **sparkles** were **stuck** in my deodorant. My armpits were reflecting light like disco balls! **"**

that's hot!

"Our entire family celebrates Hanukkah together. We have this big dinner, and my mom lights these pretty **candles** in the center of the table. While we were eating, I reached over to get some food—but my shirt caught on **fire**! I freaked out and got so scared that I ripped off my shirt and started beating out the flames! I put the fire out—and **realized** I was standing in front of my **whole** family wearing only a bra and a skirt! I got out of there—**fast**!"

fashion

fashion statement

"It was 'What the Heck Are You Wearing Day' at school and I was pumped up about my **crazy** outfit. I wore super-skinny gray jeans with red shorts, an ugly green shirt with a loose tank top, and over that, another spaghetti-strap tank. I **also** had on a big gold belt, dozens of hair clips, and two headbands. When I **walked** into school I saw that I was the only one dressed up—it was the **wrong** day! All day, everyone was asking me 'What the heck are you wearing?'"

fashion

seeing red

"I was sitting on my crush's lap one day. When I stood up, I was **mortified** to find a red blotch on his jeans, right where I was sitting! I started **stammering** about my period and how sometimes a regular tampon isn't enough. He looked really **confused**, then looked at his leg and said, 'Uh, Morgan, I spilled **ketchup** on myself at lunch.' I was totally humiliated—I had gone on and on to him about girl problems for nothing!"

no tanks

"I'm pretty flat-chested, so I don't wear bras that often. One day at school I wore this cute little wool **sweater**, and underneath it, I had a loose tank top. We were getting ready to go outside for lunch, and it was warm out, so I took off my sweater. Unfortunately, the tank top **stuck** to my sweater as I was pulling it up, and it came right off! I flashed my **entire** class! After that, there was this one **jerk** who would tell me, 'Hey, I saw your tit!'. Ugh!"

fashion

precious metal

66

On a school trip, we all had to go through this metal detector. I kept setting off the **alarm**, but I couldn't figure out why. The guy started waving the detector wand over me when it **finally** hit me. I was wearing this new thong that had a little metal ring in the **back**! It was bad enough to tell him, but then he made me turn around so he could **scan** my butt! **Everyone** from my school knew what had happened.

99

body wash

"All of the cheerleaders were having a car wash to raise money, but I had forgotten my swimsuit and had to **borrow** my friend's too-small bikini. It seemed to be holding up just **fine**, until I got done washing this super-cute guy's car—and he handed me an instant **photo** of my exposed nipple pressed up against his car window! I couldn't believe what a jerk he was for doing that, but my friends totally laughed!"

fashion

sole train

" I was trying to get on the train this morning, and people can be **animals** when it comes to being first on board. While **rushing** to get on, some jerk totally steps on my shoe and kicks it right off of my foot—and it **landed** on the tracks. The train then plowed over my cute black flat, and I was left half-barefoot, hopping around the nasty, **dirty** train station. It was seriously my worst fashion moment ever. **"**

big waist

"One day my best friend and I went to Old Navy. We went to the dressing rooms to try on these cool black **skirts**. They were really **weird**. They were way huge around the waist, and they didn't have ties or zippers or anything to adjust them. We walked out of our dressing rooms to show each other how **bizarre** and ugly the skirts were when the dressing room attendant said, 'Those are supposed to be worn **over** your shoulders, not your hips!' They were ponchos!"

fashion

riding high

" My friends and I went to this Western line-dancing place and saw a mechanical bull. I had to try it. When it started **moving**, it felt like my butt was moving in and out of my super low-rise jeans! My friends told me nobody noticed. Later, I went to the other side of the club and saw a **gigantic** screen showing a video of the bullriding. And there I was, with my larger-than-life naked butt playing **peekaboo** with the whole room. Everyone was laughing. "

fashion

the lowdown

" One day me and my mom were shopping together. I picked out a couple pairs of **jeans** and headed to the dressing room. The second pair I tried on were **super** low-rise. I opened the door to model for my mom and there were some **hot guys** standing behind her. Then, my mom said, 'Honey, if those jeans were any **lower**, your pubic hair would stick out!' I could **not** have been more mortified. "

under-oohs

"
I was a finalist at my town's science fair, and we were all called onstage to sit facing the **audience**. I was **nervous**, so I was crossing and uncrossing my legs a lot. When the winners were announced, I wasn't one of them. I was pretty upset, but it got **worse** when my ex came up to me and said, 'Perfect view!' I didn't know what he was talking about, but then **another** guy said, 'I like your undies!' Every time I uncrossed my legs, the **whole** audience was peeking up my skirt!
"

fashion

off her chest

" I landed the lead part in our school play this year. I wore this long, strapless dress for one scene, and I borrowed a bra that was a little too **big** for me from my sister to go under it. During the **second** show, I bent over to pick up a prop, and my bra slid down to my lower stomach! It looked like I had **alien** boobs sticking out of my tummy! The whole audience—including the other actor onstage—was **giggling**. I was *so* embarrassed! "

fashion victim

"I was late for school and walked into my first class 10 minutes **after** the bell. I was pretty embarrassed, but at least I looked hot in my **new** V-neck Banana Republic sweater. Then this guy I liked **whispered**, 'Hey, I'm glad you made it to class today!' I was **pleased** that he noticed me—until he **shouted** out, 'Too bad you didn't look in the mirror before you left the house. Isn't the V-neck supposed to be in the **front**?' All the guys started to laugh—I was horrified!"

fashion

wedgie walk

"I threw a party in my basement and invited my friends and my longtime crush. I borrowed my friend's wedge **shoes** so I looked extra nice. At one point I was coming down the stairs and I **slipped** and fell down the whole flight of stairs. I landed really hard right on my butt and **screamed**, 'Ouch! My butt!' The entire party went silent for a moment as everyone stared. Then they all started **laughing**— my crush was almost in tears. At my next party I made sure I wore flats."

index

A

a holiday hit, 74
a star is born, 164
about to dye, 86
adult content, 124
all fired up, 68
anatomy 101, 176
art lover, 194

B

baby mama, 185
bad santa, 133
ballbuster, 122
bare essentials, 204
best in show, 203
big waist, 243
blowout, 60
board walk, 227
body talk, 139
body wash, 241
bogeyman, 134
boogers, 60
book drive, 199
bottoms up, 215
breakthrough role, 171

bright idea, 87
bus wrecked, 210
butt double, 174

C

cake walk, 161
candid camera, 63
catch of the day, 13
check, please, 88
cheesy question, 92
class jean-ius, 196
clear view, 38
closet case, 20
clothes call, 216
crash n burn, 102
cream of weep, 187
crushing blow, 12
curtain call, 160
cyber slipup, 37

D

dinner disaster, 73
dog run, 166
double stuff, 218
double talk, 101

dramatic scene, 182
draw a crowd, 212
drowned out, 147
duffle shuffle, 144

E

excess baggage, 222
exchange policy, 19
eye browse, 59

F

face-off, 155
facedown, 141
fake numbers, 55
fall sport, 49
farting, 73, 107, 146, 156
fashion statement, 235
fashion victim, 249
festival of fright, 76
fire and brimstone, 83
fish, go, 14
fishing, 13
flip out, 90
floor manager, 186
food fight, 62
foot bawl, 50
football, playing, 12
foreign exchange, 84

French kiss, 173
full moon, 188

G

gas, passing, 23
getaway car, 17
girls on film, 125
go fish, 14
gotta jet, 23
guessing game, 98
gym class hero, 48
gym period, 184
gym-nauseam, 25

H

half-baked, 152
hands down, 180
handy snacks, 148
he says/she says, 217
heart attack, 205
heel no, 208
hide-and-peek, 31
ho, ho, oh, no, 67
hot flash, 209
hunger pains, 116

I

icy reception, 71
in a bind, 200

in the cards, 111
intimates moment, 230

J

jersey error, 169
jet fuel, 156
juicy fruit, 228
just snot right, 130

L

lady in red, 165
language lesson, 192
light my fire, 105
lip service, 108
locked out, 140
lost and found, 35
love hurts, 168
lovesick, 30
lowdown, 246

M

making moves, 43
maxi pads, 24
merry mistake, 66
miss spoken, 197
mistaken identity, 126
mistle toe, 106
mixed messages, 36
mobile chat, 29

monitor mishap, 70
movie pass, 16
mr. sensitivity, 54
mr. wrong, 114
mud bath, 40
multitasker, 172
my two scents, 45

N

no tanks, 239
noisemaker, 177
northern exposure, 226
nosy neighbor, 106
numbers game, 34

O

off campus, 132
off her chest, 248
off her rocker, 112
off the rack, 32
oh, brother, 99
ornamental oops, 46
out of shape, 154

P

paper trail, 22
parent trap, 104
park place, 149

pass out, 94
passed up, 179
pepped up, 192
photo madness, 128
plumber bummer, 24
poor baby, 225
pop quiz, 202
pop stop, 97
potty talk, 153
precious metal, 240
present tense, 145
private matters, 77
private performance, 223
puddle jumper, 52

R

riding high, 244
rise and shine, 234
roadside attraction, 110
royal flush, 115

S

santa pause, 146
say cheese, 120
scene and heard, 191
seat warmer, 181
seeing red, 238
send-off, 44

shaken up, 100
shakin' it up, 131
she bangs, 57
shoplifter, 232
shower issues, 20
showering off, 138
sight unseen, 113
slipup, 233
snack attack, 78
sole train, 242
sounding off, 58
special delivery, 158
speech therapy, 190
speed bump, 93
spitting distance, 51
stage wrong, 198
stopping traffic, 28
strung out, 224
surprise surprise, 56
sweet cheeks, 211
swing state, 178

T

tampons, 19
tennis lessons, 26
thanks a lot, 72
that's hot, 235
the deep end, 42
the real feel, 121

thin ice, 159
tissue issue, 18
toilet paper, 22
toss-up, 229
total phon-y, 55
total relaxation, 150
treasure hunt, 135

U

under-oohs, 247
undressed to impress,
    214
urine luck, 85
urine trouble, 127

V

very personal shopper,
    82
vomiting on your crush,
    25, 30

W

wedding brawls, 79
wedgie walk, 250
wet and wild, 142
what a bummer, 221
what a scene, 80
wind breaker, 170
wrestle mania, 96
wrong call, 39
wrong note, 91
wrong solution, 136

Y

you got served, 26

Z

zip up, 220